VLADIMIR KABAKOV was born in Irkutsk, in Siberia. After leaving school, he did his military service in the Soviet Army and worked at the University of Irkutsk. He has been a carpenter, geologist and teacher and was the sports coach and director of a St Petersburg youth club. He is also a writer and journalist. His latest Russian book, *They say that Bears Don't Bite*, was published in 2007. Vladimir now lives in London and returns to Russia every year. He is married with two children.

PRODEEPTA DAS was born in Cuttack, in eastern India. He is a freelance photographer and author whose pictures have been published in over 30 children's books. In 1991 *Inside India*, which he also wrote, won the Commonwealth Photographer's Award. Prodeepta's books for Frances Lincoln include *P is for Pakistan, Prita Goes to India, K is for Korea, We are Britain!, Geeta's Day, I is for India, J is for Jamaica, Kamal Goes to Trinidad, P is for Poland, B is for Bangladesh, When I Grow Up* and *S is for South Africa*.

For my wife Sue, who has loved Russia and Russian culture for many years –V.K.

To Grisha and Volodya in St Petersburg, Tolya and Igor in Irkutsk,
Lena on the Trans-Siberian Express, Dr Victor Yudin in Amur, Janetta, Yvonne and Judith
at Frances Lincoln for their support, and my family in London
for forgiving my long absences in Russia –P.D.

First published in Great Britain and the USA in 2011 by
Frances Lincoln Children's Books, 4 Torriano Mews,
Torriano Avenue, London NW5 2RZ
www.franceslincoln.com

First paperback edition published in 2013

A catalogue record for this book is available from the British Library.

ISBN 978-1-84780-427-3

Set in FFScala

Printed in Shenzhen, Guangdong, China by C&C Offset Printing Co., Ltd in November 2012

1 3 5 7 9 8 6 4 2

R is for Russia

Vladimir Kabakov
& Prodeepta Das

F
FRANCES LINCOLN
CHILDREN'S BOOKS

Author's Note

I was born in Siberia, not far from the legendary Lake Baikal. Ever since I was a boy I have been going on summer and winter trips in the forest with my friends. I have lived and worked in different parts of Russia and have come to love the enormous country that is my home: the vast forests, the *steppes,* the mountains and valleys, the rivers, lakes and seas, the bustling towns and cities. Russia is so vast – it stretches more than ten thousand kilometres from Europe in the West to the Pacific Ocean in the East. When it is morning in Moscow, it is already evening in Vladivostock!

As you turn the pages of this book, you will see many of the things which make Russia so special: its fine palaces and churches, its musical and cultural traditions, its magnificent scenery and spectacular winter landscapes – and you will also see the food we eat, the sports we play, as well as ordinary Russian people going about their everyday lives.

I hope that one day you will visit Russia and see some of this wonderful country for yourself.

Владимир Кабаков

Aa

is for Astronaut. Russia was the first country in the world to send a human being into space. In April 1961 Yuri Gagarin made his record-breaking flight on board the spaceship *Vostok 1*. He spent 108 minutes in space and orbited the earth once. The first woman in space was Valentina Tereshkova, in June 1963 on the spaceship *Vostok 6*. She was in space for nearly three days and orbited the earth 48 times.

Bb is for Ballet. Russia's most famous classical ballets are *Swan Lake, The Nutcracker* and *The Sleeping Beauty,* all with music by Pyotr Ilyich Tchaikovsky. Our ballet schools teach children from age five right up to eighteen. They dance alongside adults in theatre performances.

**C c** is for Chess, a popular game with both adults and children. Some of the greatest world chess champions are Russian. During the summer you will see people sitting outside playing chess in parks and gardens throughout the country. Many children belong to chess clubs and take part in tournaments.

Dd is for Dacha or country cottage. Most of us live in towns, but we love to spend time at our dacha. Often it doesn't have running water, so we have to fetch water from the well or village pump. Out in the garden we grow fruit and vegetables.

Ee is for Easter eggs. We celebrate Easter by giving each other eggs – either real eggs dipped in dye, or wooden eggs painted with flowers, churches and colourful patterns. The jeweller Peter Carl Fabergé created the most amazing Easter eggs for the Russian royal family, like the one below right. Made of gold and precious stones, it opens up to reveal a surprise inside!

 is for Fairy Tales. Our favourite character is the witch Baba Yaga, who lives in a house built on chicken's legs and flies around in a pestle and mortar terrifying people! Some of the best fairy tales were collected and written down by the poet Alexander Pushkin and illustrated by the artist Ivan Bilibin – like this picture illustrating an adventure of the Tsarevitch, son of the Russian king.

G g is for Gymnastics. Many Russian gymnasts have become Olympic champions. Promising young gymnasts go to classes at the Moscow Children's Palace of Culture and Sport and spend hours practising their routines. Even if they don't end up as Olympic gymnasts, their gym lessons help them to grow up fit and healthy.

H h is for Hat. You will need one to keep you warm during the winter. We recommend a traditional *shapka-ushanka* with flaps that you can pull down over your ears in very cold weather. You will also need a thick coat and some warm boots. When you are snug and warm from top to toe, the Russian winter will hold no terrors for you!

Ii is for Icon, a religious portrait which you will see in churches and homes all over Russia. Some of them date back more than 600 years. They are usually painted on wood and show scenes from the Bible or the lives of saints. Our most precious icons have ornamental metal covers and are sometimes studded with jewels.

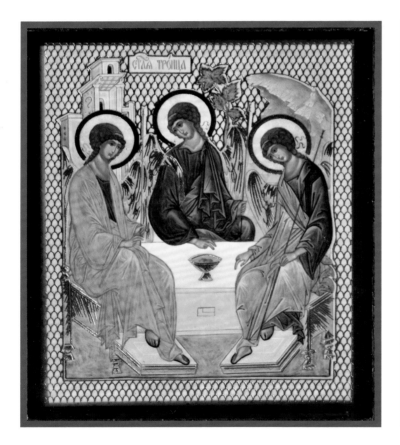

Jj is for Journey. Russia is so vast that if you want to visit another town, you will probably have to make a long journey. The Trans-Siberian Railway from Moscow to Vladivostok, a journey of over 9,000 kilometres, lasts six days and takes you through amazing changes of scenery. Your train compartment becomes your sitting-room and at night you are lulled to sleep by the gentle rocking of the train.

is for Kremlin or fortress. Our most famous kremlin is in Moscow, where the government meets. Inside, you will see some wonderful churches and cathedrals as well as the Armoury, full of the weapons and jewellery of Russia's rulers who once lived inside the Kremlin.

is for Lake Baikal, "the Pearl of Siberia". The oldest, deepest and clearest freshwater lake in the world, Baikal has over 300 different rivers flowing into it and one river, the Angara, flowing out again. The lake contains a huge variety of plants and animals, including a kind of seal found only in Baikal. In winter the entire lake freezes.

 is for Matryoshka. Hidden one inside the other, this traditional set of wooden dolls is simple to take apart, but not so easy to put together again! The dolls usually show a cheerful woman, but you can also buy Matryoshki with the faces of famous people such as politicians.

 **N n** is for North. A huge area known as the Tundra stretches up to the Arctic Ocean. The earth is frozen most of the year and the sea freezes in winter, making it ideal for skiing and sledging. Home to reindeer, bears, arctic foxes and polar bears, the region is always dark in winter and light in summer – when it is known as "the Land of the Midnight Sun".

Oo

is for Orthodox Church. The blue and gold domes of Russian Orthodox churches sparkle in the sunshine and their bells call people to prayer. Inside, the walls and ceilings are often painted with frescoes and hung with icons. On festival days the priest and worshippers carry icons in procession round the church.

Pp is for Pancakes, eaten on special occasions such as Maslenitsa when we celebrate the end of winter and the coming of spring. For us, the shape of the pancake symbolises the sun. We like eating our pancakes with sour cream, melted butter, jam or caviar.

 is for Queen or Tsaritsa (pronounced *t-zar-rit-sa*). We have not had a royal family since 1917, but once Tsars and Tsaritsas were important in our history. The most powerful Tsaritsa was Catherine II, "Catherine the Great", who sat on the Russian throne for over thirty years in the 18th century. She built some splendid palaces, among them the Catherine Palace outside St Petersburg (above left).

Rr is for Russia, the biggest country in the world. The Russian Federation stretches from the Baltic Sea in the west across Europe and Asia to the Pacific Ocean in the east, and from the Arctic Ocean in the north to the Black Sea in the south. Much of Russia is covered in forest and open spaces or *steppes*, but we also have mountains, deserts, rivers and big cities including our capital, Moscow. During her history of splendour, revolution and change, Mother Russia has produced some of the greatest scientists, sportsmen and women, writers, dancers and composers in the world.

S s

is for Samovar. Fancy a cup of tea? Then we'll light the samovar. It keeps the water hot so that you can have tea whenever you like, and to make sure the tea doesn't get cold, there is a stand on top to hold the teapot. Lighting a samovar is not easy, though! Many people now use electric samovars or kettles instead.

T t

is for Tiger. The Siberian tiger is the largest wild cat in the world and the most dangerous predator in eastern Russia. There are not many left, so there is a ban on hunting them. They feed on wild boar and deer, and rarely attack humans. Seeing one of these beautiful wild animals is an experience you will never forget.

U is for Underground Railway. The Metros in Moscow and St Petersburg are so beautifully decorated that walking through them is like being in a palace or museum. The walls and columns are often made of coloured marble, and you will see paintings, mosaics, sculptures and even glittering chandeliers hanging above some of the platforms!

is for Volga. The Volga is Europe's biggest river, rising in the Valdai Hills north-west of Moscow and flowing out into the Caspian Sea at Astrakhan. It was once an important trade route and many major cities grew up along its banks. You can still travel along the Volga by steamship, but only in summer – for three months every year most of the Volga is frozen.

is for Winter Palace, a beautiful building in the heart of St Petersburg built for the Tsar and his family. One side stretches along the banks of the River Neva while the other looks out on to Palace Square and the Alexander Column. After the Russian Revolution of 1917, the Winter Palace became a museum and now houses one of the world's greatest art collections.

X x is for Xop or choir (pronounced *hor*). Children sometimes take part in recitals alongside adults, often dressed in traditional costume. They sing classical pieces, folk and even pop songs. On festival days such as the May Day holiday, families will often sit around the table after their meal and sing, accompanied by the guitar, piano accordion or a traditional stringed instrument called the *balalaika*.

Y y

is for Youth Club. Whatever you like doing – sport, dancing, sewing, crafts – you are sure to find others who share your interest at a youth club and improve your skills there. Young people often go to the youth club after school, at the weekend and during their school holidays.

Z z

is for Zenit. If you are a football fan, you must have heard of Zenit! Together with its rival Dynamo, it is one of Russia's most popular football teams. Many young Russian footballers dream of playing for one or other of these two famous clubs.

MORE TITLES IN THE WORLD ALPHABET SERIES
FROM FRANCES LINCOLN CHILDREN'S BOOKS

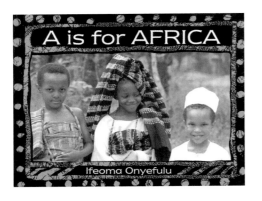

A IS FOR AFRICA
Ifeoma Onyefulu

From Beads to Drums to Masquerades, from Grandmother to Yams, this photographic alphabet captures the rhythms of day-to-day village life in Africa. Ifeoma Onyefulu's lens reveals not only traditional crafts and customs, but also the African sense of occasion and fun, in images that will enchant children the world over.
"Delightful and highly original." *Junior Education*

B IS FOR BANGLADESH
Urmi Rahman
Photographs by Prodeepta Das

From Dhaka to Jamdani, from Crocodile to Rickshaw, here is a photographic alphabet introducing Bangladesh. The People's Republic of Bangladesh, once part of India, is a young country with an ancient history and centuries of tradition. Rivers criss-cross the country, feeding the rice-fields and sometimes flooding the Bay of Bengal. Yet the Bangladeshi people are amazingly resilient and welcome everyone with a smile.

C IS FOR CHINA
Sungwan So

From Abacus to Lantern, from Jade to Wenzi, this photographic alphabet introduces young readers to the rich culture and natural beauty of China. Sungwan So's variety of colourful images is a tribute to a traditional society whose people have faced challenges of revolutionary change with courage and strength.

Frances Lincoln titles are available from all good bookshops.
You can also buy books and find out more about your favourite titles,
authors and illustrators on our website: www.franceslincoln.com